Freedom Press

Mines and Boobytraps - Vietnam
1969 Special Issue

They are provided for informational purposes only.

ISBN-13: 978-1511501989
ISBN-10:
1511501987

FAIR USE ASSERTION

Professional Knowledge Gained from Operational Experience in Vietnam, 1969, Special Issue, Mines and Boobytraps

U.S. Marine Corps

PCN 140 124300 000

DEPARTMENT OF THE NAVY
Headquarters United States Marine Corps
Washington, DC 20380-0001

20 July 1989

FOREWORD

1. PURPOSE

Fleet Marine Force Reference Publication (FMFRP) 12-43, *Professional Knowledge Gained from Operational Experience in Vietnam, 1969, Special Issue, Mines and Boobytraps*, is published to ensure the retention and dissemination of useful information which is not intended to become doctrine or to be published in Fleet Marine Force manuals. FMFRPs in the 12 Series are a special category of publications: reprints of historical works which were published commercially or by the U.S. Government Printing Office and are no longer in print.

2. SCOPE

This reference publication complements existing training manuals on small-unit tactics, patrolling, weapons, mines and boobytraps, and leadership. Written by a multitude of Marines during the Vietnam War, this volume is an excellent compendium of lessons to be learned from the Marine Corps' experience in 1969. It is enthusiastically recommended to all junior officers, SNCOs, and NCOs who will profit from the principles presented.

3. CERTIFICATION

Reviewed and approved this date.

BY DIRECTION OF THE COMMANDANT OF THE MARINE CORPS

M. P. SULLIVAN
Major General, U.S. Marine Corps
Deputy Commander for Warfighting
Marine Corps Combat Development Command
Quantico, Virginia

DISTRIBUTION: "11.9"

MINES AND BOOBYTRAPS

CONTENTS

ENEMY MINE WARFARE

INTRODUCTION

The history of mine and boobytrap warfare is almost as long as the history of
war itself. Although these devices were
once considered an unfair and cowardly
manner of fighting an enemy, nations continued to develop and employ mines and
boobytraps because they provided an effective and simple means of inflicting
casualties upon an enemy force.

During the war with France, 1946-1954,
the Viet Minh used improvised explosive
mines and boobytraps effectively against
the French forces. The VC/NVA have continued to improve upon these techniques
and are employing mines and boobytraps as
an effective weapons system against free
world military forces in SVN today. The
number of Marine casualties, perhaps
better than any other example, illustrates
how effective the enemy is with these
devices. Marines landed in force in SVN
during March 1965 and during the first
months of fighting approximately 65-75
percent of all Marine casualties were
caused by mines and boobytraps. Much has
been learned about the enemy's methods of
employing mines and boobytraps since March
1965, but despite this knowledge, Marines,
at an alarming rate, continue to become
casualties as a direct result of enemy
mines and boobytraps. During 1968, 37.7
percent of all Marine casualties were
caused by the accidential detonation of a
mine or boobytrap. In other words, more
than one of every three Marines killed or

wounded in SVN becomes a casualty as the result of a mine or boobytrap. Although a great many detection means, ranging from intricate electronic devices to specially trained dogs, have been developed, experience has shown that <u>an alert Marine</u>, aware of what to look for and where to look, is <u>the most effective</u> detection device.

The information contained in this book is intended to make each Marine aware of the ways which the VC/NVA use mines and boobytraps and to describe the means to effectively protect one's self and unit from these devices. To aid in this objective, mines and boobytraps frequently used by the VC/NVA are identified and described.

Study this issue; the information in it can save lives -- yours and your fellow Marines'.

******

ENEMY DOCTRINE

Although modified by past guerrilla warfare experience in Vietnam, VC/NVA mine
warfare doctrine continues to closely parallel that of the Chinese Communist Army.
Extensive deliberate minefields have not
been encountered in Vietnam. Rather, the
enemy employs mines singly or in clusters
to achieve his purposes.

In areas occupied and protected by free
world forces, the enemy employs mines to
delay and disrupt the use of roads and
paths and to cause the allies to divert
forces to guard and clear those routes. In
addition to the threat to military traffic
and lawful civilian movement, the free
world personnel and equipment employed in
patrolling the roads and in detecting and
removing mines are prime targets.

In contested areas where friendly offen-
sive operations or patrol activities are
conducted, the enemy employs mines and
boobytraps to inflict casualties, delay
and channelize movement, and damage or
destroy equipment.

******

ENEMY SOURCES OF SUPPLY

The enemy uses a very limited number of
modern machine-produced mines. The major-
ity of enemy mines are handmade by the VC
using U.S. duds, discarded ammunition and
equipment, and materials thrown away by
U.S. forces as trash. Ninety percent of
all the material in enemy mines and boobytraps is of U.S. origin (see fig.1). Of
all the explosive devices produced locally
in VC mine factories, 95 percent are antipersonnel boobytraps.

3

Figure 1.--Enemy equipment captured
by Marines on sweep operations in ICTZ.
Note US M-26 grenade in center of
picture. Other grenades are locally
produced using C-ration cans.

All dud ammunition is a source of enemy
supply. After airstrikes and artillery
and mortar missions, enemy salvage teams
make sweeps to collect duds. Lighter
ordnance is carried away to preparation
areas; large bombs and projectiles are
broken down and stripped on the spot. In
some cases the larger duds are rigged as
boobytraps where they have fallen. This
is especially true when the enemy feels
the strike or fire mission was a preparation for an infantry attack.

However, dud ammunition is not the only
source of enemy supply. Carelessly discarded ordnance of all sizes and in any
quantity is collected by enemy salvage
teams. Mortar rounds, rockets, LAAW's,

grenades, and small arms ammunition abandoned to lighten the load (or improperly
secured and lost by fast-moving Marines)
have value as the explosive element in
boobytraps. Even a single M16 round
ejected to clear a stoppage can be used
by the enemy.

Additionally, materials discarded as
trash and improperly destroyed such as
ration, ammunition, beer and soda cans,
batteries, waterproof packaging materials,
bandoliers, etc., provide the enemy a
valuable source of supply to support his
mine warfare operations. These items
have, on numerous instances, been employed
successfully against Marines and their
equipment. Thorough police of friendly
positions upon departure and complete
destruction of trash are mandatory to deny
the enemy this source of supply.

******

VC MINE FACTORIES

Primitive VC mine factories are usually
located in the areas they supply. Great
care is taken in the camouflage and dis-
persal of these facilities. Usually constructed underground, effort is made to
disperse the workshops and storage throughout a series of tunnels. These limit
destruction by working accidents or free
world force artillery, air and naval gunfire and protect against discovery. As
important as concealment of the mine
factory, is the mobility of its personnel
and equipment. Even while the mine factory
is being settled in one position, new
positions are being prepared for rapid
displacement. Rarely does a mine factory

5

remain in one place any longer than a few
weeks. There is no distinct pattern of
movement. Factories have been known to
return to previous positions even after
that position has been discovered and
destroyed by Marine forces.

NVA-trained engineers provide the
skilled nucleus for the enemy mine factories, but supervision and labor are
primarily VC. The typical output of a
local VC mine factory is about 135 mines
and explosive devices per month.

******

ENEMY TACTICS

ANTITANK AND ANTIVEHICULAR MINING

As we improve in our ability to detect
mines, the enemy counters with new twists
such as increased use of boobytraps
attached to a basic mine to create casualties among mine-clearing personnel;
larger mines buried deeper with reduced
activation pressure; and pressure electric
detonators with offset devices to explode
mines under vehicles. Command-detonating
mines are normally used in densely populated areas and pressure-type devices in
less populated sections. The heaviest
mining is along lines of communications
near fixed installations.

The enemy makes every effort to avoid
repeating practices which, when analyzed,
could indicate a pattern. Therefore, the
VC/NVA doctrine stresses where to use
mines, not how. Listed below are a few of
the kinds of places where enemy antitank
and antivehicular mines may be found:

●Road junctions and the areas in the
vicinity of the road near the junction,

6

with all the mines set to detonate simultaneously.

- Bridges and the approaches 5 to 15 meters from the bridges.
- Old wheel and tread tracks in the road, with care taken to duplicate the track after mine emplacement.
- Underneath roads, tunneling in from the shoulders.
- Potholes in the road.
- Areas recently cleared by free world military forces. The enemy replaces the mines that have been taken out.

ANTIPERSONNEL MINES AND BOOBYTRAPS

Enemy tactics in emplacing antipersonnel mines and boobytraps differ from those used in antitank and antivehicular mining only by where they put them. Locations most commonly used by the VC/NVA to emplace antipersonnel mines and boobytraps are:

- Narrow passages.
- Paddy dikes.
- Trail junctions.
- Hedgerows and tree lines.
- Tunnels and caves.
- Fence lines and gates.
- Tree branches overhanging trails.
- Likely CP sites.
- High ground and ridgelines.
- Shady areas.
- Stream fords.
- Wells and natural watering points on streams and rivers.
- Likely helicopter landing zones.

▶ Remember: Any place a Marine frequently walks, takes cover, rests, or draws water is a likely location for enemy antipersonnel mines and boobytraps.

7

COUNTERMEASURES

Countermeasures are those actions, both tactical and nontactical, that can be taken by units and/or individual Marines which reduce the mine and boobytrap threat. Countermeasures decrease the enemy's ability to emplace mines and boobytraps or limit their effectiveness if they are emplaced.

NONTACTICAL COUNTERMEASURES

The most effective way to counter the enemy's mine and boobytrap threat is to destroy this threat at its source; i.e., the elimination of the VC/NVA mine and boobytrap factories and the sources of supply for these factories.

Every effort must be made to locate existing enemy mine and boobytrap factories and to determine likely locations for future factory sites. Hoi Chanhs, POW's and captured documents must be carefully processed because, with skillful handling, they provide vital information on factory location sites. Once found, existing factories and future locations must be made unusable.

More important than neutralizing the enemy's mine and boobytrap factories, is the denial to the enemy of the source of supply with which he operates these factories; i.e., unexploded U.S. ordnance, discarded equipment and improperly destroyed trash. The fact that U.S. ordnance and salvageable trash falls into enemy hands can be traced to several factors:

9

▷ Unexploded Ordnance

The first factor and an important source of unexploded ordnance for the enemy is provided by the free world military force's employment of air, artillery and naval gunfire support. Some ordnance items fail to detonate, become a "dud" and provide a potential mine or boobytrap. All Marines who employ fire support should consider this fact in the employment of supporting arms, and be careful not to call for fires in excess of what is required to accomplish the mission.

▷ Abandoned Munitions

The second factor, another important source of explosive materiel supply for the enemy's mine and boobytrap operations, is abandoned or lost munitions. The following examples, if allowed to occur, will assist the enemy in his efforts:

- Overstockage. A unit overstocks ammunition and then is required to move on short notice with only a basic load. The remaining ammunition is left on the abandoned position.

- Ammunition Handling Procedures. A unit attempts to turn in excess ammunition to an ASP (ammunition supply point) and is refused due to inefficient disposal procedures.

- Abuse of Ammunition. A unit discards ammunition considered unserviceable because of dirt, tarnish, mud or other avoidable conditions or minor imperfections.

- Loss in Transit. A helicopter sling breaks on an ammunition resupply mission and all or a portion of the load is scattered across the countryside.

10

◊ Improperly Destroyed Trash

The last factor, but far from least
important to the enemy's mine and boobytrap program, is his source of supply from
friendly trash. All items considered
unusable by free world forces must be com-
pletely destroyed or properly disposed of.
Figure 2 shows one example of the results
of an improperly policed friendly area of
operations. Discarded C-ration/soda cans
are also commonly used in a type of boobytrap which is constructed with an M26
grenade. The safety pin is removed and
the grenade is put in the can. When the
can is disturbed, the grenade slips out,
the spoon pops and the grenade detonates.

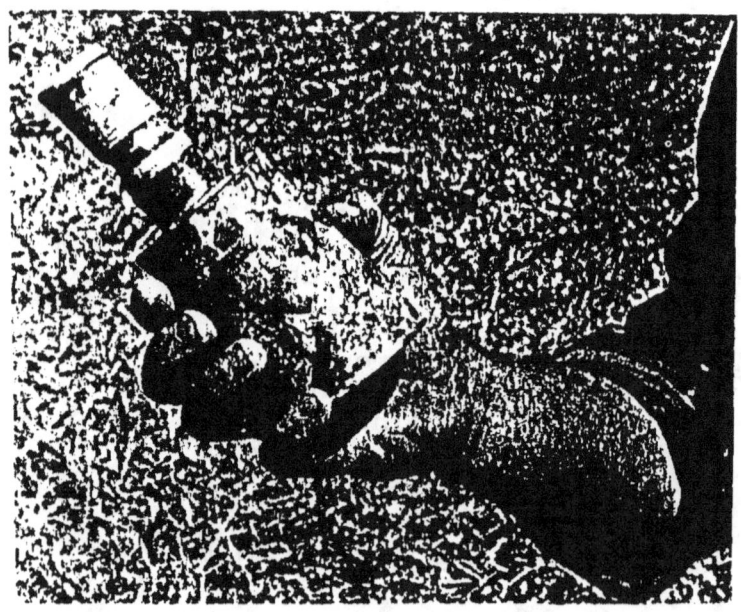

Figure 2.--Shown is a VC grenade made
from locally available materials including a carelessly discarded "Coke"
can.

11

*****

The VIP (Volunteer Informant Program) has proved to be an increasingly effective countermeasure to the enemy's mine and boobytrap efforts. This program rewards Vietnamese individuals who turn in dud and abandoned munitions. Continued emphasis on this program will significantly decrease the enemy capacity to employ U.S. ordnance against free world forces. (See fig. 3.) During one period, 188 of 259 payments in the III MAF area were made to children who turned in explosives suitable for the manufacture of boobytraps. To ensure that the effectiveness of VIP reaches its full potential, it is the responsibility of every individual Marine and each Marine unit to give VIP their complete support.

Figure 3.--Shown here is the VIP (Volunteer Informant Program) in action. Articles on ground have been turned in to Marines by local villagers.

TACTICAL COUNTERMEASURES

Tactical countermeasures employed by
Marine units are very effective in reducing the enemy's capability of emplacing
mines or boobytraps if such countermeasures
are aggressively planned and executed. Unit
commanders have several tactical measures
at their disposal, including the employment
of sophisticated electronic devices. They
are:

- Employing portable ground radar and
seismic intrusion devices.
- Maintaining a constant physical presence throughout the TAOR to include outposting of key roads. This is the most
effective tactical countermeasure, but
sometimes difficult to achieve because of
the number of Marines required to ensure
good coverage.
- Conducting aggressive patrolling.
- Conducting reconnaissance patrols to
verify S-2 intelligence reports.
- Employing scout-sniper teams.
- Conducting small unit cordon and
search operations in coordination with
Vietnamese units/police.
- Employing H&I fires over roads or
over specific areas.
- Employing small stay-behind patrols
dropped off unnoticed from units passing
near a road.
- Paving or oiling dirt roads.
- Patrolling and outposting on and
near roads.
- Employing Kit Carson Scouts. Using
the native ability of the Kit Carson Scouts,
coupled with their knowledge of the area
of operations and VC activities, can prove
highly useful in locating devices. During

October 1968, Kit Carson Scouts found 229
mines and boobytraps in the III MAF area.

●Scout Dogs. Using specially trained
dogs (see fig. 4.) to detect the scent left
by the individual emplacing a mine or
boobytrap. This scent is detectable 1-4
days after emplacement. Since boobytraps
are generally emplaced shortly after initi-
ation of friendly operations, the chance
of discovery by dogs is good. A trained
dog will use his vision to detect tripwires
and unnatural elements, and his hearing to
detect sound waves created by tripwire
vibration. Many dogs detect a tripwire
when it touches the body hair of their
forelegs or chest. Most are agile enough
to back away before it is tripped. Of 119
dogs killed in SVN since January 1967,
only seven were killed by boobytraps.

Figure 4.--Specially trained dogs
such as the one shown here have proven
extremely valuable in detecting enemy
mines and boobytraps.

14

INDIVIDUAL COUNTERMEASURES

Individual countermeasures are those measures each and every Marine can take to diminish the effectiveness of a mine or boobytrap device which has been emplaced, and is found or is accidentally detonated. This can be accomplished through physical protective measures, detection and destruction measures, avoidance of explosive devices, and through application of immediate action when an explosive device has been accidentially detonated.

▷ Physical Protective Countermeasures

The individual Marine can take these steps to reduce the effectiveness of enemy mines:

- Wear body armor and helmet.
- Sandbag vehicle flooring. When possible, place a heavy rubber mat over sandbags to reduce secondary fragments such as shrapnel, sand, stones and pieces of sandbag.
- Keep arms and legs inside vehicles to achieve maximum protection from sandbags.
- Maintain proper distance from other personnel.
- Don't travel alone.
- Don't pick up or touch what appear to be attractive "souvenirs". The VC/NVA prey upon the natural curiosity of Marines and their desire to take home a souvenir. ▶Beware: That "souvenir" is most likely a boobytrap.

▷ Detection Countermeasures

Once emplaced, a mine or boobytrap must be found before it causes multiple casualties through accidental detonation by

15

a Marine. Unfortunately, too many boobytraps are discovered only after they
explode. It is imperative that detection
techniques be stressed. Detection may be
by:

● Visual inspection. At present, the
best mine and boobytrap detector in the
Marine Corps is an alert and observant
Marine. Each Marine must know the areas
in which boobytraps and mines are normally
found and be alert for things which "just
don't look right." Examples are:

● Mud smears, mudballs, dung, or a
board on the road.
● Apparent road repair, new fill or
paving patches, ditching or culvert work.
● Wires leading away from the side of
the road.
● Tripwires across the trails; along
shoulders of roads at likely ambush sites;
across the most accessible route through
dense vegetation; at fords, ditches and
across rice paddy dikes.
● Terrain features which do not appear
natural. Cut vegetation dries and changes
color; rain may wash away covering material
and cause an explosive device to sink
leaving a surface depression; a covered
device may appear as a mound.
● Suspicious items in trees, branches,
or bushes.
● Markings used by VC/NVA to indicate
the location of a mine or boobytrap.

● Probing. Suspicious spots must be carefully probed with a probe or bayonet.

● Mine detectors. Mine detectors are
designed to assist the individual Marine
in a detailed, deliberate sweep of a specific area, usually a road. Particular

16

attention must be given to the time factors
of the individual sweeping situation, since
overhasty opening of a road can mean an
ineffective sweep and quite possibly
destruction or injury to vehicular traffic
and personnel. The average sweep rate
varies from almost nothing to about 5 m.p.h.
depending, of course, on the proficiency
of the team and the number of contacts
encountered. In using detectors, certain
considerations must be kept in mind:

●Graveled roads make it difficult for
the AN/PRS-4 detector to discriminate
between real and false targets.
●Metallic debris, such as can tops,
small arms ammunition cases, and metal
fragments from artillery rounds fired over
roads at night to discourage mine laying,
make it difficult for the AN/P153 detector
to discriminate between real and false
targets.
●The tendency for the enemy to bury
mines deeper than designed detection depths,
and to deliberately plant metallic debris
in the road, calls for additional caution
in the use of detectors.
●Operator fatigue. Consideration must
be given to the fatigue experienced by
operators after 20 minutes of wearing
detector earphones. This condition can be
delayed to 1 or 2 hours by wearing earphones
over the helmet so that 2 to 4 inches exist
between ear and phone. This also permits
the operator to hear a verbal alert for
an ambush.

● Use of the Buddy System. This system
is not only useful in training inexperi-
enced Marines, but also provides an extra
margin of safety to the individuals who
employ it. Two Marines working together,
in the same area, have the advantage of

increased detection capability, mutual reassurance, and shared knowledge.

▷ Destruction Countermeasures

Once detected, mines and boobytraps must be marked and/or destroyed in place by the discovering person or unit to prevent accidential detonation by a following unit or individual Marine. Considerations for destruction are:

- Mines and boobytraps should not be moved unless absolutely necessary and then only by qualified EOD or engineer personnel. Many boobytraps are themselves boobytrapped, and if disturbed will detonate the associated device.
- Explosive devices should be destroyed by engineers. If engineers are not available, then devices may be destroyed by selected qualified personnel within each unit.
- Mines and boobytraps may be destroyed or neutralized by use of grappling hooks, demolitions, and artillery fires. The LVTE linecharge and the LVTE with plow-shaped mine excavator (figs. 5 and 6) should be considered for use in areas of high mine density.

▷ Avoidance Countermeasures

Strict application of training and careful planning of movements through danger areas will enable unit commanders and individuals to reduce casualties by simply avoiding the explosive devices. The unit leader must analyze from the enemy's viewpoint each area through which he intends to move his men. He must ask himself the question, "If I were the enemy, where would I put the boobytrap?" This question can and should influence both administrative

18

Figure 5.--The LVTE firing its organic
linecharge to clear mines.

Figure 6.--The LVTE with its plow-shaped
mine excavator.

19

and tactical movements and is a factor to
be considered in the scheme of maneuver
during an attack. Some suggested means
for avoiding mines and boobytraps are:

●Stay off trails, footpaths, cart
tracks, or other likely routes of travel
as much as possible. Vary routes used to
villages and key terrain features. Use of
the same route twice is an invitation to
the enemy to employ boobytraps. Keep the
VC/NVA guessing as to which route will be
used next.

●Move where local inhabitants move.
These people know the location of most
mines and boobytraps and will avoid these
areas. In a village, stay near the vil-
agers and watch which buildings they use.
Use Vietnamese as guides whenever possible.
Have sufficient money on hand to pay for
information on mine and boobytrap locations
and support VIP.

●Avoid patterns. Constantly change
direction of movement. Check times of
departure and return of patrols to ensure,
for example, that all daylight patrols
don't return before supper and all night-
time patrols depart after supper. Avoid
the repeated use of the same bivouac areas.

●Maintain intervals of 15 meters between men and 100 meters between men and
tracked vehicles. In view of the fact
that the effective casualty radius of the
M26 grenade is 15 meters, and that two or
more casualties are suffered for each
boobytrap grenade accidently detonated,
the maintenance of proper interval is <u>most</u>
important.

●Move slowly. Rapid movement generates
carelessness. A unit must be allowed sufficient time to move to its objective.

●At times the enemy will show themselves
only when they want to be seen. When

pursuing the enemy, be especially alert for deliberately emplaced boobytraps on the axis of advance.

●Artillery and mortar fires near and in the area of operations will not only discourage boobytrap emplacement, but will also neutralize devices by sympathetic detonation, overturning and burying emplaced mines, and rupturing tripwires. Employment of these fires beside a road, before and during a road sweep, will discourage command detonation of road mines.

●At all times, a lightweight stick (bamboo) or a slender steel rod can be helpful if used to feel for tripwires.

●Mark detected mines and boobytraps so those following may avoid them.

●Helicopters can be used to extract a unit which finds itself in a heavily boobytrapped area.

●At times, the flanks of a road are boobytrapped out to 250 meters as an obstacle to road sweep security teams. Tanks, preceding the infantry, can detonate these boobytraps. When trafficability permits, tanks moving off and parallel to the road sweeps can also reduce tank road-mining incidents. Random selection of tank travel between road and adjacent terrain will keep the NVA guessing as to the actual route the tank will take.

●When on roads, stay in the well-used portion and off shoulders.

●Follow the tracks of the vehicle ahead. If there is no vehicle ahead, stay out of the ruts.

●Avoid holes, depressions, and objects lying on the road.

► Remember: A boobytrap too easily detected can be a ruse resulting in detonation of other explosive devices emplaced nearby.

21

* * * * * *

Immediate Action To Take When and After an Explosive Device Is Tripped

It is recognized that little reaction time exists once the detonation chain starts. The maximum delay for the M26 and foreign grenades ranges from 4 to 9 seconds. If the delay element has been modified, the minimum fuse delay can be less than 1 1/2 seconds. However, since the time available cannot be predicted, certain immediate action can assist in reducing casualties and the degree of personal injury.

◊ Immediate Action

FIRST: Be alert for the "pop" of the exploding cap, the tug of the tripwire, or the warning of another Marine.

SECOND: Sound a warning so that others may take cover.

THIRD: Drop to the ground immediately.

Immediate action is designed as an instinctive reaction based on minimum fuse delay. When using it also remember:

● Do not attempt to outrun the explosion. The 800 fragments of the M26 grenade have an initial velocity of over 5000 feet per second. During the available delay, however brief, an individual can best remove himself from the cone of the explosion by dropping to the ground. He must assume a minimum delay in every case.

● If possible, when dropping to the ground, present the smallest target to the force of the explosion by pointing the feet in the direction of the charge.

● All those nearby should drop to the ground when the warning is sounded.

22

•Do not immediately rush to the aid
of Marines wounded by mines or boobytraps.
Frequently there is a second boobytrap in
the vicinity of the first. The man near-
est each casualty should carefully clear
his way to the wounded individual and
render first aid. Under no circumstances
should the unit leaders or others crowd
near the wounded men.
    •Conduct a brief but careful search
for other explosive devices in the immediate vicinity before moving on.
    •If a device is tripped and does not
explode, follow the same immediate action
and then blow it in place.

******

UNIT TRAINING

    We have discussed preventive counter-
measures, tactical countermeasures and
individual countermeasures. Simply real-
izing that these countermeasures exist
isn't sufficient. It is imperative that
every Marine becomes knowledgeable of and
proficient in the execution of the countermeasures discussed. This task can be
accomplished through an aggressive and
comprehensive unit and individual training
program. Such training should emphasize:

    •Wearing of helmets and body armor.
    •Dispersion between men.
    •Alertness.
    •Visual detection techniques.
    •Operation of electronic detection
equipment.
    •Demolition training which enables
Marines to destroy explosive devices in
place.
    •Employment of the buddy system.
    •Avoidance of patterns.
    •Immediate action procedures and action
to take subsequent to the detonation of an
explosive device.

23

ENEMY MINE INDICATORS

If the enemy emplaces mines or booby-traps in the vicinity of villages or in areas where he moves or expects to move, he often indicates the location or direction of the explosive devices in some manner. The VC/NVA may not always follow the examples in this publication in absolute detail, but as a general rule, the indicators are usually found in a regular pattern such as sticks or stones in a line or sticks placed on or in the ground. This regularity of pattern is the danger signal (see fig. 7). Any arrangement of sticks and stones which appears unnatural indicates a strong possibility of the presence of

Figure 7.--Note the row of rocks on top of bridge beam at the foot of the bridge. This is typical of the warning signs used by the VC/NVA to warn of their mining activities.

25

mines and boobytraps. The illustrations
which follow are examples of marking patterns indicating the presence of mines
and boobytraps which have been encountered
thus far in SVN.

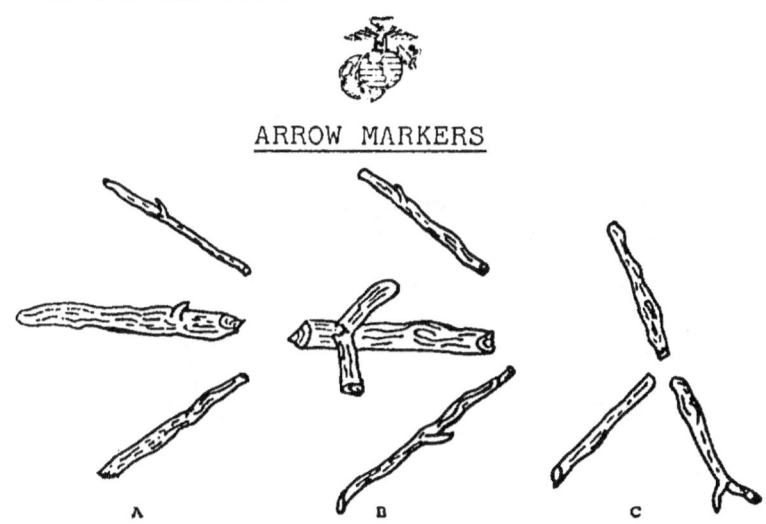

ARROW MARKERS

A. Three sticks are placed on the trail in
the form of an arrowhead. The important
thing to remember is that the point of the
arrow does not always point in the direction
of the boobytrap. The symbol can only be
considered as a means to identify an area
as being boobytrapped.

B. A variation of the three-stick arrowhead
shows a fourth stick. Again, no definite
pattern has been established as to direction
or the reason for the fourth stick (usually
broken). But it does mean boobytraps in
the area.

C. The "Y" arrangement is sometimes found
farther down the trail from the arrowhead
indicating the limit of the danger area.
No pattern or specific distance has been
established.

BAMBOO RECTANGLE MARKER

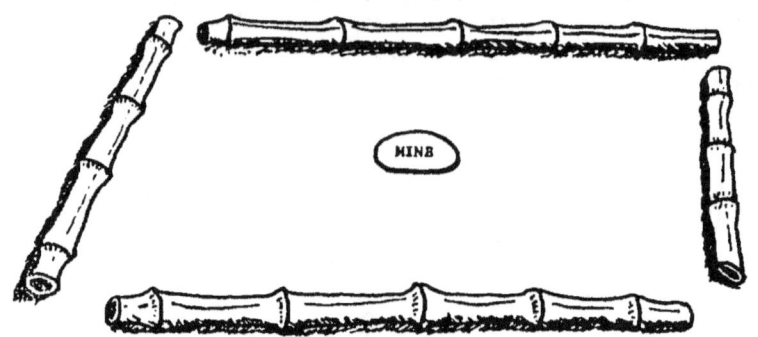

As shown, this marker usually indicates a boobytrap within the square. Most of these symbols found have been laid out with bamboo 18 to 42 inches in length.

BAMBOO MARKER

A piece of bamboo 6 to 8 inches long is stuck in the ground at an angle of 45 degrees. Generally, boobytraps can be expected along the axis of the bamboo in either direction.

27

BAMBOO TRIPOD MARKER

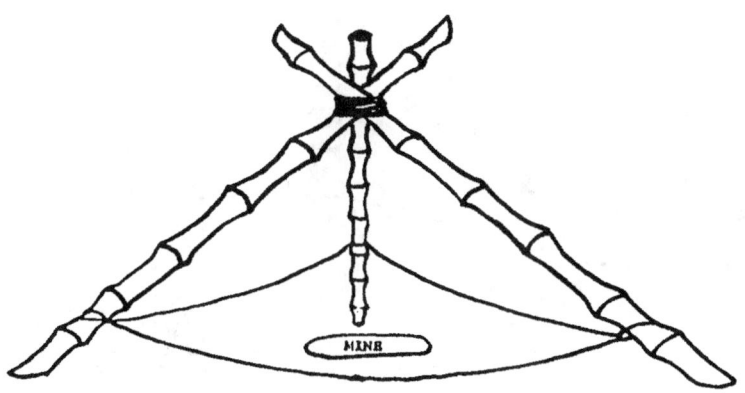

The bamboo tripod consists of bamboo,
usually about 18 inches long, tied together to form a tripod. Wire, vines,
cord or string is wrapped around the legs
near the bottom to hold the tripod in
place. This device has been found directly
over punji pits, boobytraps, and mines.

BROKEN BUSH OR STICK MARKERS

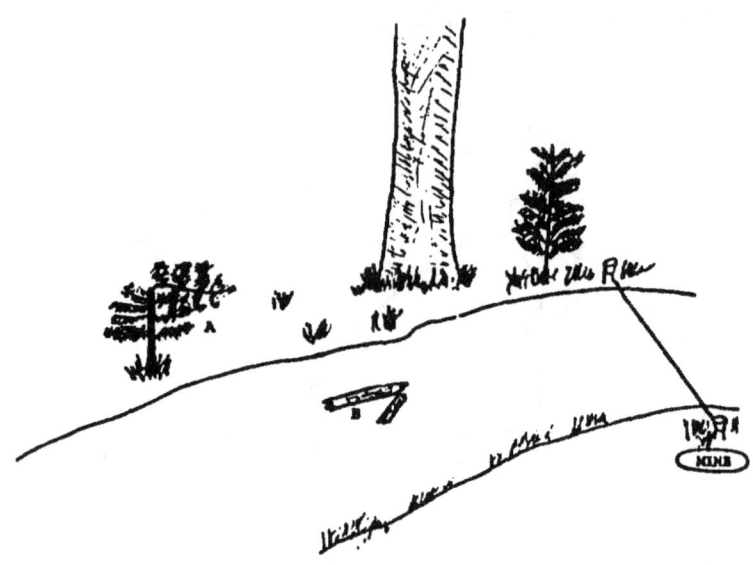

A. The enemy has been known to break the tops of small saplings and bushes pointing the broken part in the direction of the boobytrapped area. Usually mines and boobytraps are planted 50 to 100 meters from this marker.

B. A stick or length of bamboo broken at a right angle and lying across the road or trail may mean an enemy mine or boobytrap 200 to 400 meters ahead.

BANANA LEAF MARKERS

A banana leaf or other similar leaf is
folded down the center with a thin stick
approximately the thickness of a toothpick
woven through in two places. In addition
to marking mines, this may indicate an
ambush area. There is no pattern as to
location or distance of mines or ambushes
from this marker.

PARALLEL STICK MARKER

Short sticks or lengths of bamboo laid
parallel to a road or trail usually mean
the road or trail is free of mines or
boobytraps.

GROWING GRASS MARKER

MINE

Growing grass is sometimes tied to form four growing sheaves of grass. The tied sheaves form a square of about 6 feet. The mine is buried or concealed in the center of the square.

TRAIL MARKERS

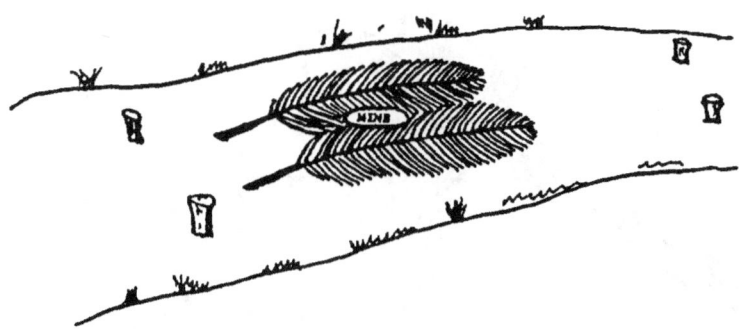

These devices have been used extensively together. The mine or boobytrap is placed (buried) under two large leaves. In front and to the rear, at no special distance, stakes are driven. The markers have also been used independently of each other at times.

FORKED-STICK MARKER

A forked stick is driven vertically
into the ground and another stick is laid
into the fork with the elevated end pointing to the danger area. Distance to
explosive device is unknown. This sign
may also indicate enemy direction of
movement.

ROCK MARKERS

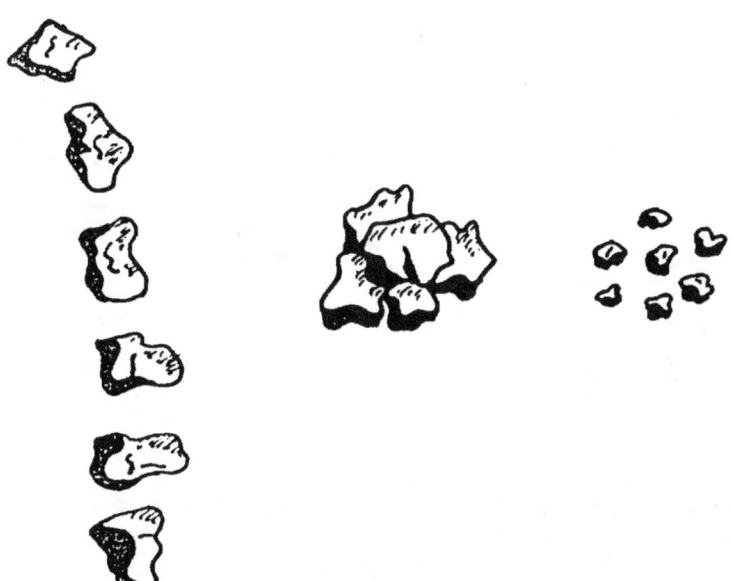

Various formations of rocks and small
stones are used to mark boobytrapped areas.
No pattern of distance or location has
been established.

34

SPACED-STICK MARKER

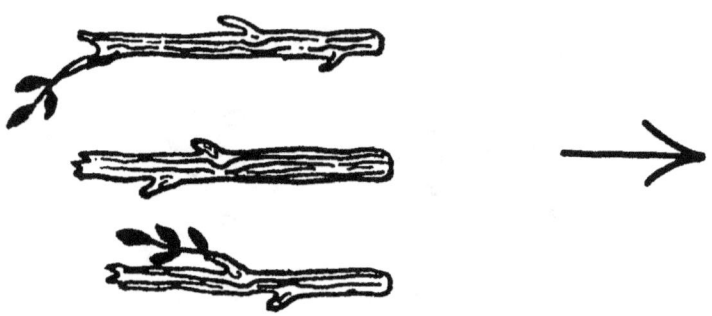

Three sticks, one on each side of a
road or trail and one in the middle,
usually mean the road is not to be used.
A mine or boobytrap is usually 200 to
400 meters from the marker. Stones have
been used in the same manner.

TRACK MARKER

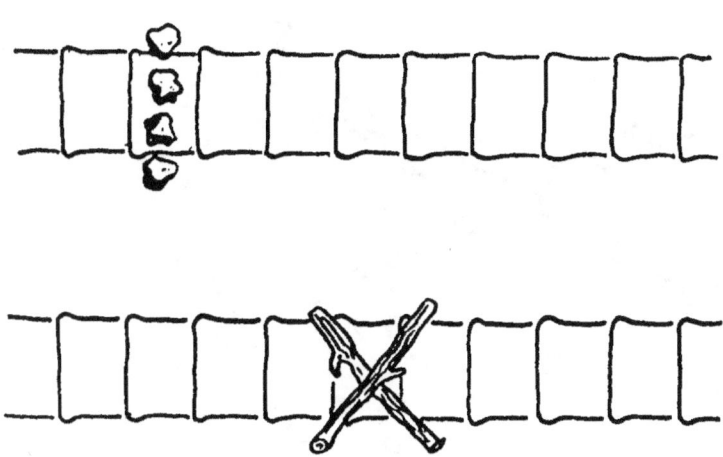

The enemy has capitalized on our habit of following old vehicle tracks by placing mines in these tracks. Mines are sometimes marked with crossed sticks or an arrangement of stones. The location of the mine in relation to these markers is unknown. The mine may be under the marker or up to 400 meters farther on.

STAKES WITH X-MARKER

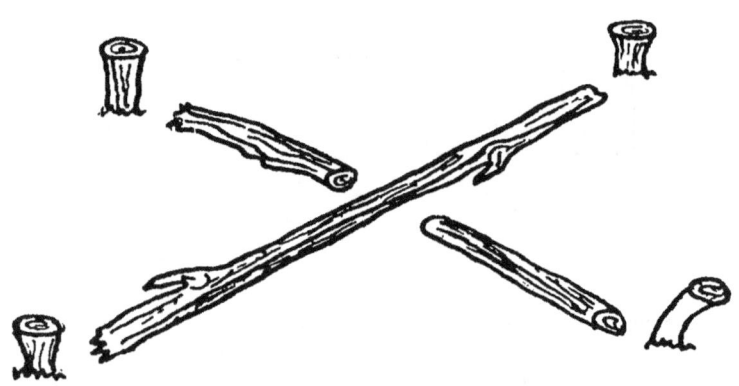

An M1A1 antitank mine with approximately
25 pounds of TNT was discovered under this
marker. The mine had been marked with
stakes at each corner and three sticks
forming an "X" over the mine.

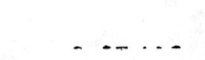

ENEMY MINES AND BOOBYTRAPS

EXPLOSIVE ANTIPERSONNEL DEVICES

Mines and explosive boobytraps employed
by the enemy against friendly personnel
are limited in type and quantity only by
the availability of explosive materials
and the imagination of the enemy. Anything that can be made to explode and
cause injury can be rigged as an antipersonnel mine or boobytrap.

Antipersonnel mines and explosive
boobytraps are very successfully employed
by the VC/NVA. Part of this success is
because Marines are not familiar with the
physical description of explosive devices
normally employed by the VC/NVA, and thus
fail to recognize them prior to accidental
detonation.

The following illustrations represent
some of the devices employed by the
VC/NVA in SVN.

MUDBALL MINE

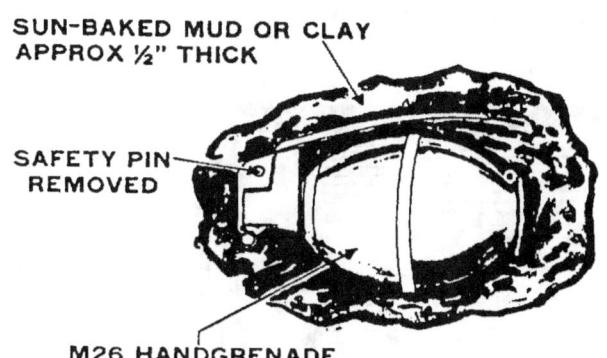

SUN-BAKED MUD OR CLAY APPROX ½" THICK

SAFETY PIN REMOVED

M26 HANDGRENADE

The mudball mine consists of a hand-grenade encased in sun-baked mud or clay. The safety pin (pull ring) is removed and mud is molded around the grenade. After the mud dries it holds the lever of the grenade in the safe position. The mudball is placed on trails or anywhere troops may walk. Stepping on the ball breaks the dried mud apart and releases the lever detonating the grenade. The U.S. M26 and M33 handgrenades have been the most commonly used grenades for this purpose although other lever-type grenades may be used.

TIN CAN ANTIPERSONNEL MINE

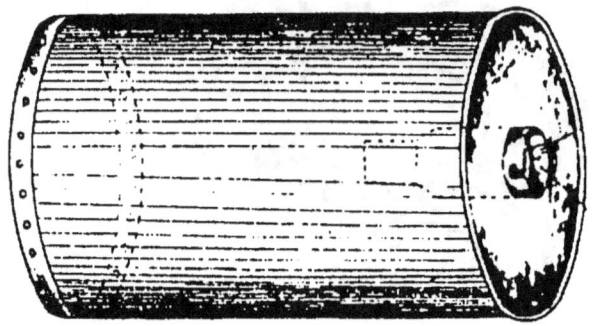

The tin can mine is constructed from
sheet metal or any discarded metal con-
tainer (C-ration, beer, or soft drink
can). The firing device for the explosive
is an improvised fuse with zero delay
action. A handgrenade fuse may be used
by removal of the delay element. The mine
functions by a tripwire attached to the
pull ring. Pressure on the tripwire pulls
the pull ring, activating the mine in the
same manner as a handgrenade.

CAST-IRON ANTIPERSONNEL
FRAGMENTATION MINE

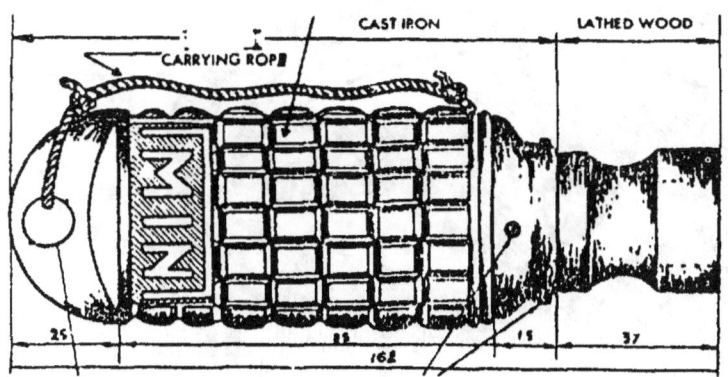

This mine, made of cast iron, resembles
a stick handgrenade with a very short
handle. The word "MIN" is often found
cast into the body. The handle houses a
pull-friction igniter. A tug on a tripwire attached to the friction igniter
will activate the fuse.

CHINESE COMMUNIST NO. 8
DUAL-PURPOSE MINE

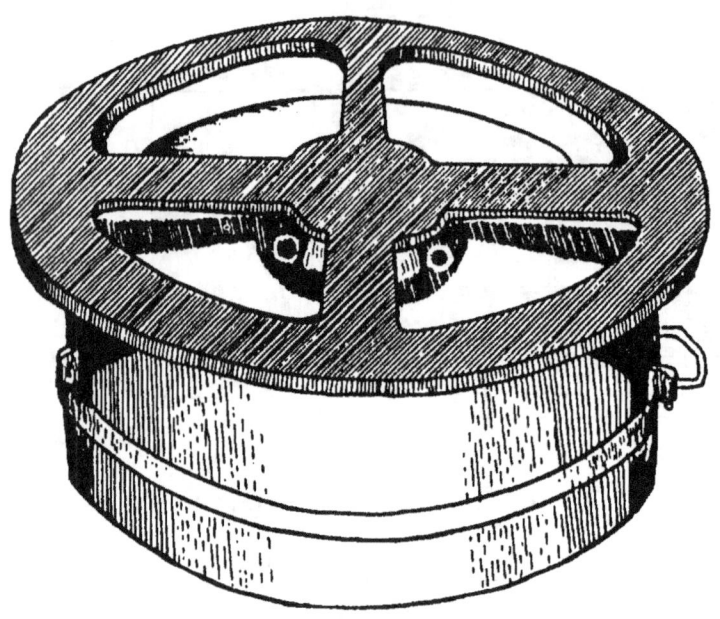

Almost identical to the CHICOM No. 4
Dual-Purpose Mine, this device also has a
double-acting fuse. Like the No.4, a
pressure of 300 pounds on the pressure
spider or a pull of 10 pounds on an attached
tripwire will detonate the mine. Slightly
larger than the No.4, this mine contains 5
pounds of explosive and has an overall
weight of 12 pounds. It is made of metal
and coated with creosote for waterproofing.

BOUNDING FRAGMENTATION MINE

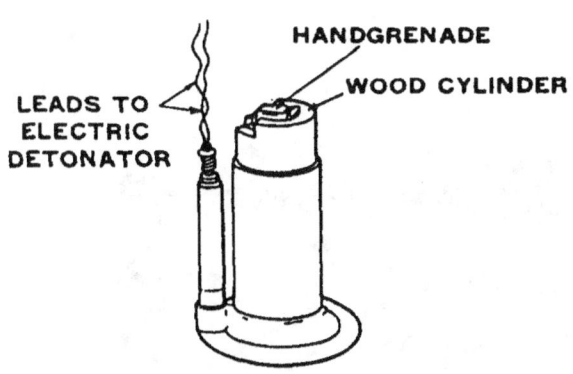

The bounding mine is improvised from expended U.S. M2 bounding mine or M48 trip-flare cases. A wooden cylinder slightly smaller in diameter than the mine case is hollowed out so that a standard grenade can fit inside. The wooden cylinder (with enclosed grenade) is then fitted into the mine case and the grenade's safety pin is extracted. When the mine is detonated, the cylinder and grenade are propelled upward. As the wooden cylinder and grenade separate, the handle flies off the grenade, activating the fuse.

VC "TOE POPPER" MINE

This mine is fabricated of cartridge cases or pieces of pipe of various sizes. It is loaded with a charge of black powder, a primer, and a variety of fragments for missile effect. When the victim steps on the mine, the igniter detonates the black powder charge and propels the fragments upward.

CARTRIDGE TRAP

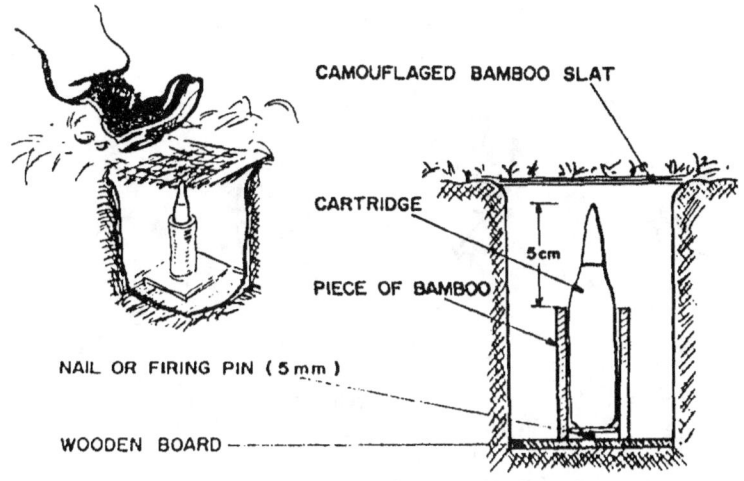

CAMOUFLAGED BAMBOO SLAT

CARTRIDGE

5cm

PIECE OF BAMBOO

NAIL OR FIRING PIN (5mm)

WOODEN BOARD

Four simple and easily obtainable components make up this mine; a bamboo tube, a nail, a piece of wood, and any small arms ammunition or M79 round. The piece of wood is used as a base. The bamboo tube is placed upright on the wooden base and a nail is driven up through the wood to penetrate the bottom of the bamboo. The cartridge is then wedged into the bamboo so that the primer is touching the point of the nail. Partially buried along a trail or path, the pressure of a man's foot stepping on the nose of the cartridge forces the primer onto the nail, firing the cartridge.

46

DIRECTIONAL FRAGMENTATION
MINE (DH-10)

Commonly referred to as a "CHICOM or
VC claymore," this mine has characteristics
similar to the U.S. M18 Claymore Mine.
Fused electrically, it is a command-detonating device designed for employment from
ambush or defensive positions. It has a
range of 150 to 200 meters and is effective
against personnel and thin-skinned vehicles.

POMZ-2 ANTIPERSONNEL MINE

BODY

PULL WIRE
INSIDE HERE

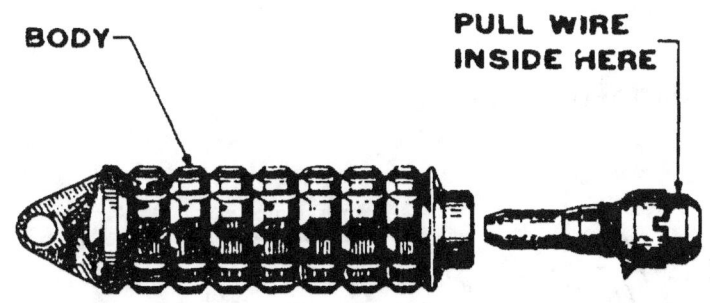

Chinese Communist copies of the Soviet
POMZ-2 mine are now being employed by the
VC/NVA. Weighing only 4.4 pounds, it is
easily carried and can be emplaced quickly.
Fused for detonation by tripwire (tension
release or pressure release), it can also
be rigged electrically for command detonation.

******

NONEXPLOSIVE BOOBYTRAPS

The idea of nonexplosive boobytraps is
as old as man. From the simple earth pit
lined with sharpened stakes to highly
sophisticated mechanisms of triggered coils
and latches, the enemy employs them all.
The principle employed is simply to use
anything that will catch the victim by
surprise.

BARBED-SPIKE PLATE

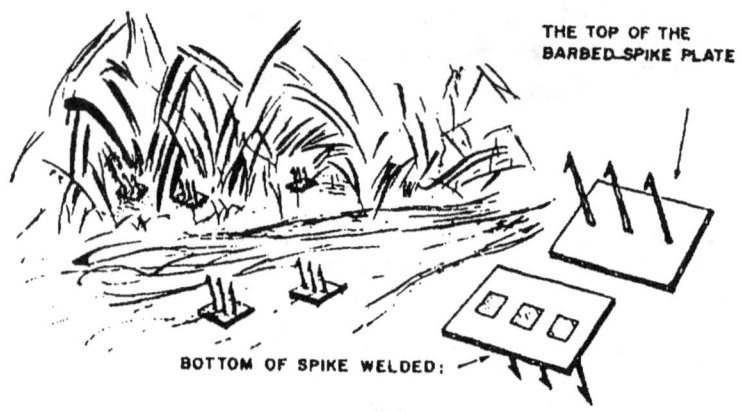

THE TOP OF THE
BARBED-SPIKE PLATE

BOTTOM OF SPIKE WELDED:

The barbed-spike plate is the basic
element of all enemy nonexplosive boobytraps. The plate, a flat piece of wood
or metal, is used as a base to fasten
any number of barbed spikes. The spikes,
ranging in length from several inches to
several feet, are fastened securely to
the base. When a man steps or falls on
the spiked plate, or is struck by one, the
spikes will penetrate, producing a
serious wound.

SPIKE TRAP BOX

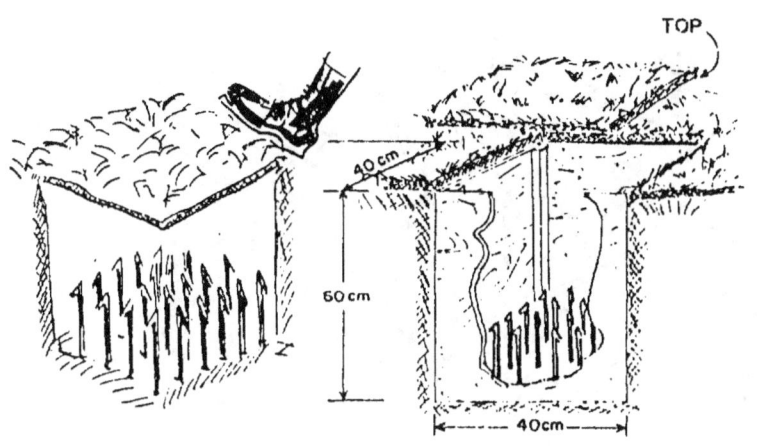

This device is a simple wooden box
made of boards joined together with four
corner posts. The box has a lightweight top
but the bottom is removed. Barbed spikes
are placed in the ground at the bottom
pointing upward. This trap is usually
set up on dirt roads and trails to take
advantage of favorable camouflage.

POINTED BAMBOO STAKES

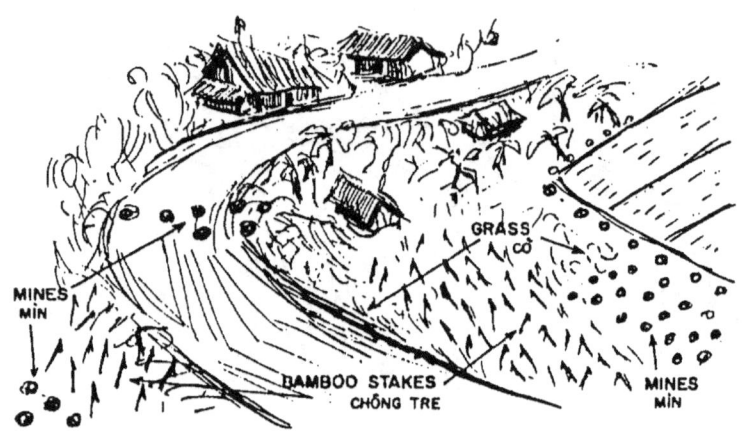

MINES
MÌN

GRASS
CỎ

BAMBOO STAKES
CHÔNG TRE

MINES
MÌN

Made of bamboo which has been sharpened, the stakes are stuck in the ground and covered with grass. When a weapon is fired or a grenade thrown, troops seek cover and are impaled.

SPIKE TRAP PIT

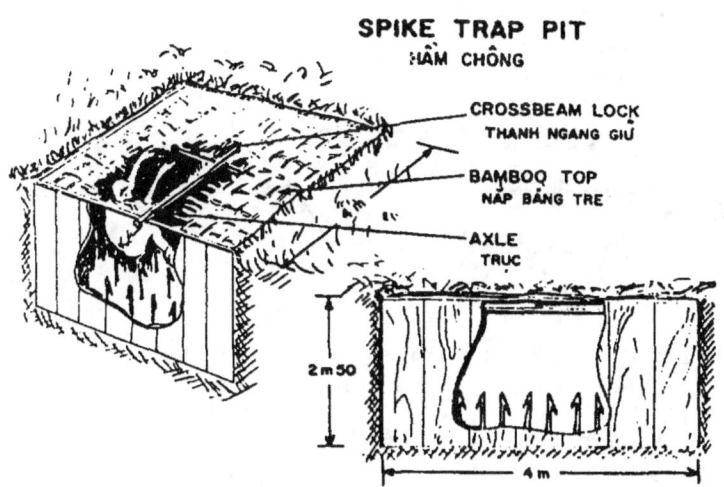

SPIKE TRAP PIT
HẦM CHÔNG

CROSSBEAM LOCK
THANH NGANG GIỮ

BAMBOO TOP
NẮP BẰNG TRE

AXLE
TRỤC

2 m 50

4 m

A trap pit is a large trap box with a bamboo top. Stakes are made of sharpened bamboo or barbed spikes and used to line the box. When a man steps on the trap he will fall into the pit. The top turns on an axle; therefore, the trap does not need to be reset to work again. The pit is often prepared as a defensive obstacle and then made safe by locking it in place with a crossbeam (so it can be crossed safely by the enemy) until the desired time of use.

52

TRAP BRIDGE

CUT AT THE MIDDLE AND COVERED WITH MUD

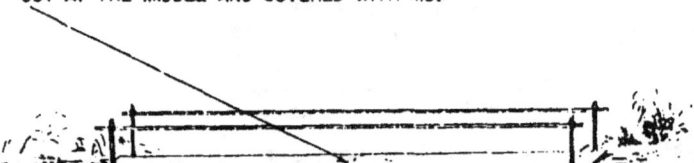

A small footbridge is partially cut in
the middle. The cut is then camouflaged
with coverings of mud, etc. Barbed spikes
or sharpened bamboo stakes are emplaced
under the cut, using the water, mud or
foilage under the bridge as camouflage.
The weight of a man on the bridge will
cause it to collapse, tumbling the victim
onto the spikes. Like the spike trap pit,
bridges can be prepared in this manner,
then braced for normal use. At the
approach of free world forces the braces
are removed.

STEEL ARROW TRAP

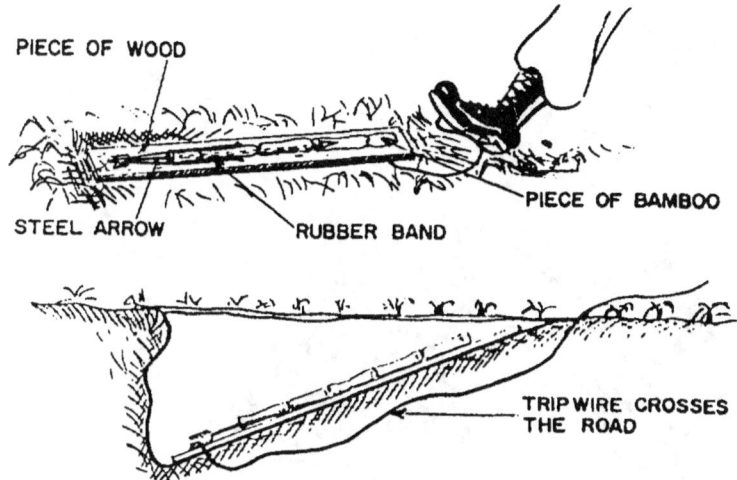

PIECE OF WOOD

STEEL ARROW RUBBER BAND

PIECE OF BAMBOO

TRIPWIRE CROSSES
THE ROAD

This trap utilizes a bamboo tube
(usually about 3 feet long) as a launcher.
A steel arrow is placed in the tube.
Using a block of wood as the bolt, a strip
of strong rubber for power and a catch to
lock the rubber strip, the device is fired
with a tripwire. When the victim trips
the wire, the latch disengages, allowing
the rubber strip to launch the arrow.

54

BAMBOO WHIP

TRIPWIRE

A strip of springy bamboo from 3 to 10 feet in length is used to make a bamboo whip. A barbed-spike plate is secured to the tip of the bamboo (or several of the spikes driven through the bamboo), and the whip is drawn back and secured. A tripwire is then latched to the whip and the wire is strung across the trail. When a man trips the wire, the bamboo is released, and whips around, striking the victim with the spikes.

ANTITANK AND VEHICLE MINES

   Mines employed by the enemy against
wheeled and tracked vehicles vary from
conventional antitank mines of foreign
manufacture to rigged duds and locally
produced explosive devices. All the in-
dustrially produced mines are of the type
fused for detonation at from 150 to 400
pounds of pressure. They are buried
slightly beneath the surface of the ground.
The enemy generally employs these mines as
designed but has varied fusing and posi-
tioning so that there is no definite pattern.

******

SOVIET ANTITANK MINE TMB-2

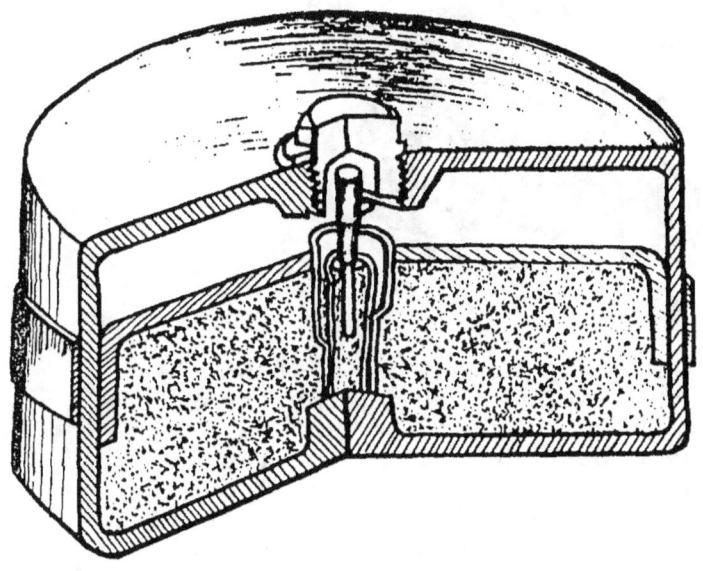

   Designed to avoid detection by a mine
detector, this mine is constructed of black
or brown tar-impregnated cardboard. It is
gauged for activation by a force of 350

pounds of pressure. Further, it can be
waterproofed by use of wood and plastic
sheeting, without losing its nondetection
characteristic. It contains 11 pounds of
explosive and has an overall weight of
15.4 pounds.

CHINESE COMMUNIST NO. 4
DUAL-PURPOSE MINE

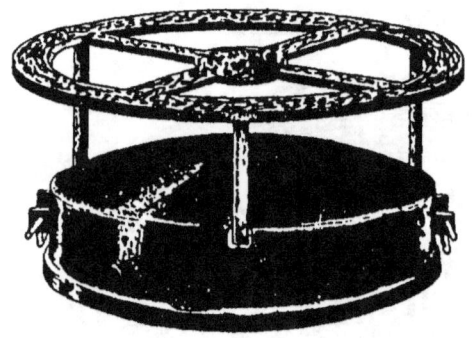

Intended for employment against both
vehicles and personnel, this mine incor-
porates a double-acting fuse that will
detonate the mine under either of two
circumstances: The first, when a load of
300 pounds of pressure is applied to the
pressure spider; the second, when a pull
of 10 pounds is exerted on a tripwire
fastened to the fuse's striker-retainer
pin. Constructed of creosoted metal, it
carries 4 pounds of explosive and has an
overall weight of about 10 pounds.

57

CONCRETE FRAGMENTATION MINE

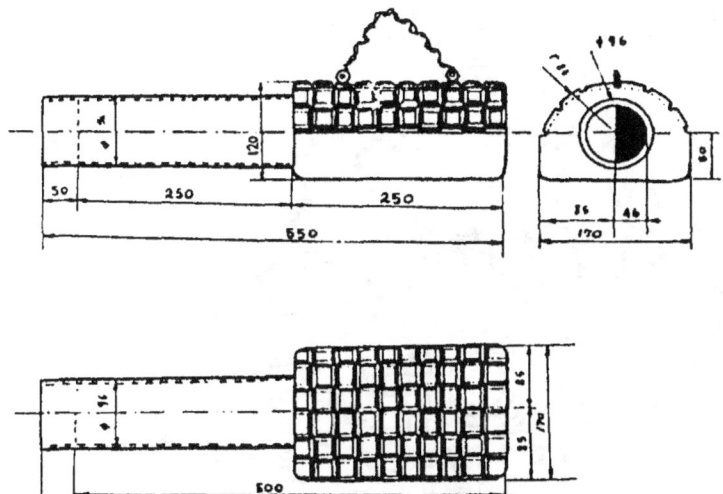

This mine is constructed of explosive encased in a cylindrically shaped concrete shell with a flat side for stable emplacement. A 2-inch-diameter pipe on one end of the mine serves as a carrying handle and detonator housing. The two swivels on top of the mine are used to tie it to an object. Usually employed as a command-detonating mine, it is equipped with an electrical firing device.

NVA CAST-IRON FRAGMENTATION
ANTITANK MINE

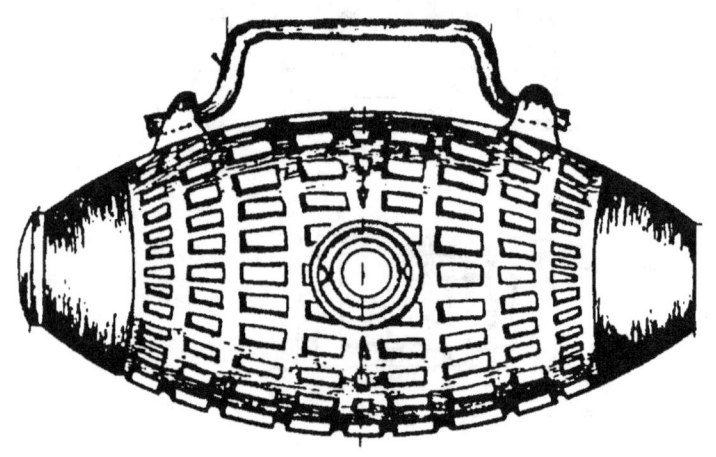

Produced in North Vietnam, this egg-
shaped mine is made of cast iron with
serrations on its outer surface. Designed
for command detonation, the mine is fused
with an electrical detonator and weighs
12 pounds.

VC MOUND-SHAPED MINE

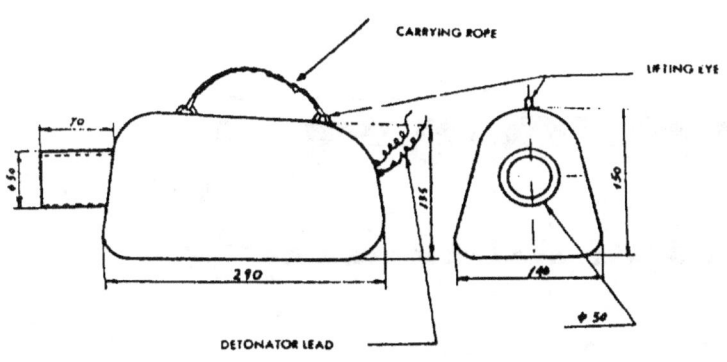

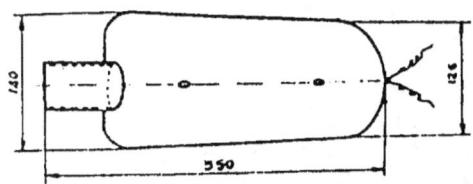

Manufactured locally in VC mine factories, this mine contains an iron-pipe detonator encased in concrete. Another command-detonating mine, it is fused electrically and weighs 13 pounds.

VC ROUND VOLUME MINE

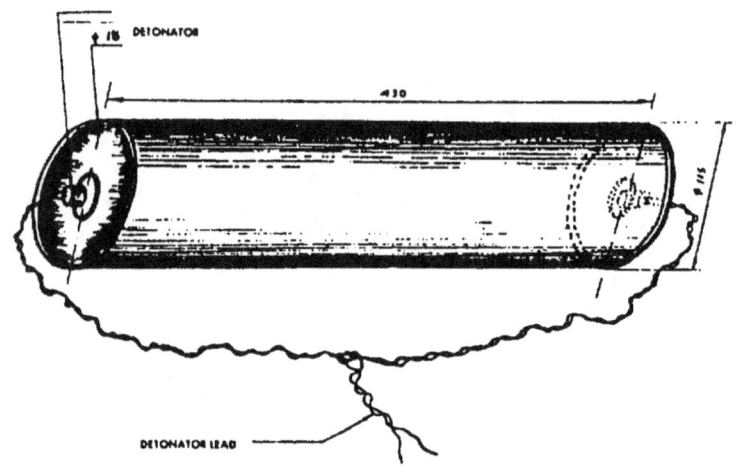

Produced locally in VC mine factories, this mine is a prototype of numerous other VC-manufactured explosive devices. Constructed of sheet metal, with welded seams, it generally weighs about 15 pounds, of which 13 pounds are explosive. Command detonated, it is fused electrically and employs two detonators, one in each end of the mine. The same principle of construction is applied to salvaged artillery shell casings, expended LAAW launchers, and most other devices using metal containers.

VC BOX MINE AND DEMOLITIONS

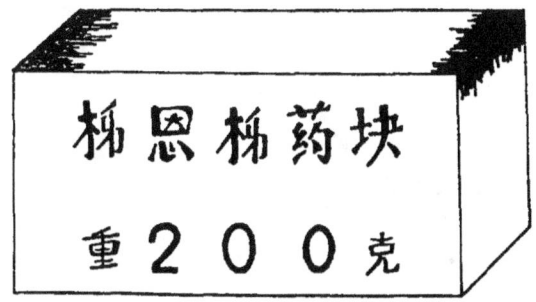

The VC box mine is constructed of wood utilizing discarded ammunition boxes or any scrap material. Mine detectors will not locate these devices. They can be water-proofed with plastic sheeting. Box mines are produced in various sizes but the most common contains about 40 pounds of explosive. The mine can be fused for command detonation or self-detonation by the use of various devices. The explosive charge is usually made up of standard Soviet or Chinese Communist 1-pound demolition blocks.

B-40 ANTITANK BOOBYTRAP

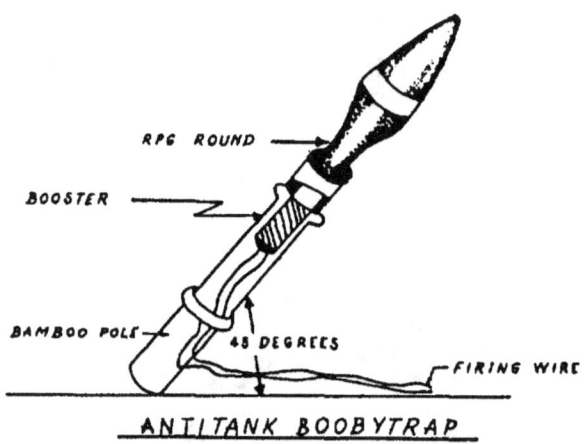

RPG ROUND

BOOSTER

BAMBOO POLE

45 DEGREES

FIRING WIRE

ANTITANK BOOBYTRAP

A length of bamboo is emplaced at an angle of 45 degrees along the shoulder of a road. A B-40 rocket is then placed in the bamboo tube and fired electrically by command detonation as the tank or vehicle crosses the line of fire.

SOVIET ANTITANK MINE TM-41

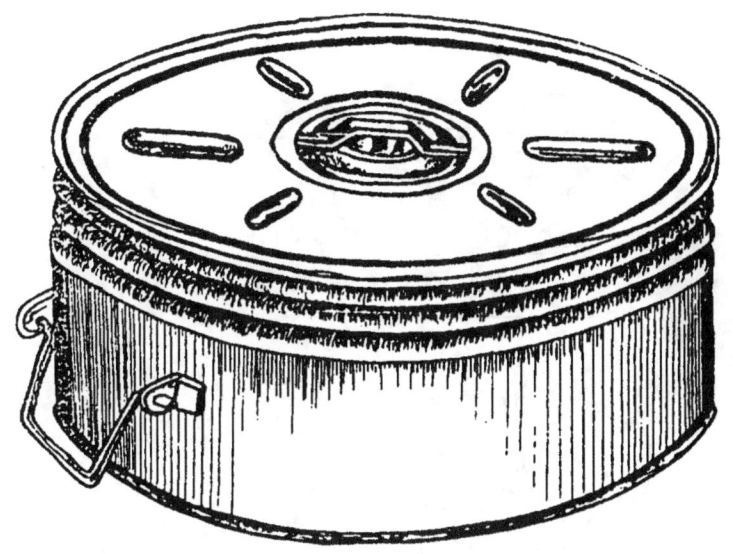

Constructed of blued steel, sometimes painted olive drab or white, the TM-41 carries an explosive charge of 8 pounds and has a total weight of 12 pounds. A force of 350 pounds of pressure on the lid will activate the firing device. With very little additional waterproofing it can remain operational indefinitely.

CHINESE COMMUNIST M1A1
ANTITANK MINE

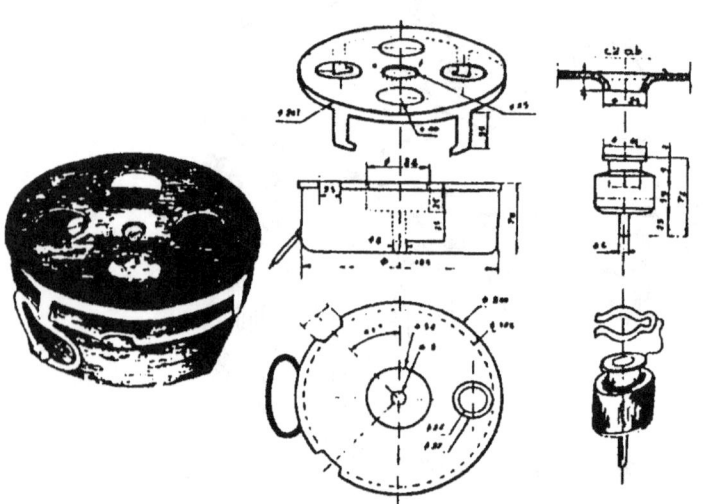

Manufactured in Communist China, this
mine is similar to and often mistaken for
a U.S. pre-World War II mine. Made of
metal, it is painted olive drab with the
yellow markings "MINE M1A1-TNT". It is
activated by 200 pounds of pressure on
the pressure plate. This mine contains
4 pounds of explosive and weighs 11.5
pounds.

ANTIHELICOPTER MINING

The degree of success that the employment of helicopters has had on restricting
and containing VC/NVA activities is evi-
denced by the enemy's efforts to destroy
or neutralize these machines. In addition
to intense ground fire, the enemy has
devised numerous helicopter landing zone
destruction systems. Such destruction
systems range from the primitive planting
of long pointed stakes to imaginative
explosive devices. Because of its design,
the helicopter is extremely vulnerable to
these devices, particulary the rotors and
airframe.

******

HELICOPTER EXPLOSIVE TRAPS

Grenades, artillery/mortar rounds, or
any other type of exploding ordnance are
mounted in trees or on the surface of the
landing zone. The explosive devices are
rigged for tripwire detonation and the

wire is strung to loosely emplaced poles.
The rotorwash of landing helicopters will
blow the poles from their loose position,
tripping the device.

******

A 13-year-old Vietnamese boy recently
claimed that the VC had forced him to
reconnoiter helicopter landing zones. The
boy was instructed by the VC to place
handgrenades in the zones with strings
wrapped around the levers, pieces of paper
attached to the free ends of the strings
and the rings (pull rings) pulled. Rotorwash from landing helicopters would then
blow the paper, unwrap the string, and
release the safety lever.